Ocean Animals

Preschool/Kindergarten

Save time and energy planning thematic units with this comprehensive resource. We've searched the 1990–1997 issues of **The MAILBOX®** and **Teacher's Helper®** magazines to find the best ideas for you to use when teaching a thematic unit on ocean animals. Included in this book are favorite units from the magazines, single ideas to extend a unit, and a variety of reproducible activities. Pick and choose from these activities to develop your own complete unit or to simply enhance your current lesson plans. So dive in! You're sure to find plenty of creative, interactive ideas that will have your youngsters hooked on learning!

Editors:
Michele M. Dare
Angie Kutzer

Artist:
Teresa R. Davidson

Cover Artist:
Kimberly Richard

www.themailbox.com

©1999 by THE EDUCATION CENTER, INC.
All rights reserved.
ISBN# 1-56234-299-1

Manufactured in the United States
10 9 8 7 6 5

Table Of Contents

Thematic Units

Thematic Units...

from The MAILBOX® magazine.

Splash!

You won't have to fish for compliments when you fill your youngsters' days with these fun fish activities. Keep them hooked with lots of arts-and-crafts projects, literature-related activities, writing opportunities, poems, a song, and a fishy foldout book.

by Lucia Kemp Henry

A School Of Swimmers

A whole school of puppet fish are irresistible bait for getting youngsters hooked on the topic of fish. To make quick work of this puppet-making project, recruit a few parent volunteers to cut out the felt pieces and assist with assembly. Have the adults use one color of felt and the body pattern on page 8 to make two fish body cutouts per child. From a contrasting color of felt, have volunteers cut out two tail pieces, one top fin, and one bottom fin for each child's puppet. When it's time to assemble the puppets, have an adult assist each youngster as he uses craft glue to glue a top and bottom fin within the perimeter of one of the fish body pieces. Then have each student run a trail of glue around the inside perimeter of his fish-body cutout, leaving the straight edge without glue. Instruct him to place the second fish body cutout on the first one. Complete the construction of the fish by having youngsters position each of the tail cutouts over the body section as shown. Glue the tails only to the body—not to each other. Set the fish aside to dry. On another day, have students use craft glue to attach button eyes and sequined tail and fin accents. Also provide fabric paints in squeeze bottles for adding finishing touches.

A Fishy Tune

Once your children are equipped with splendid fish puppets (see "A School Of Swimmers"), they'll be eager to put them to use. Make a big splash by introducing this lively song to the tune of "Did You Ever See A Lassie?" Soon each of your little ones can manipulate their puppets and imagine what it's like to swim, swish, slide, and splash through ocean currents.

Did You Ever See A Fishy?
(sung to the tune of "Did You Ever See A Lassie?")

Did you ever see a fishy,
A fishy, a fishy?
Did you ever see a fishy
Swim this way and that?
Swim this way and that way
And that way and this way?
Did you ever see a fishy
Swim this way and that?

(Repeat the song replacing the boldface word with each of these words in turn: *swish, slide,* and *splash.*)

Barry Slate

4

Five Funny Fish

Divide your youngsters into groups of five to act out this counting poem. Students are certain to get a lot of fun from saying the poem if each of them has a fish puppet for acting it out. Refer to "A School Of Swimmers" on page 4 for puppet assembly directions. As students stand in groups of five and say the poem with you, direct them to use their fish puppets or hands to illustrate the words. After asking one child in each group to sit, repeat the poem, replacing the word *five* with *four* and modifying the movements accordingly. Ask another child in each group to sit, and repeat the poem as before, substituting *three* for *four* and modifying the movements accordingly. Continue play in this manner, changing the numeral words and movements, until no students remain standing.

Five Funny Fish

Splish, splash, splish!
See the funny fish.
Five funny fish in the sea.
Swim up and down.
Swim all around.
Five funny fish in the sea.

by Lucia Kemp Henry

Move fish puppet rapidly from side-to-side.
Point to fish puppet.
Hold up five fingers.
Make up and down movements with puppet.
"Swim" puppet all around.
Hold up five fingers.

A Foldout With Fins

This whopper of a fish book will no doubt be the catch of the day. On white construction paper, reproduce pages 9–12 for each student. To make a booklet, begin by cutting around the bold outlines on each of the reproduced pages. Then color the two fish-shaped cutouts (from pages 9 and 12) as desired. Decorate each of the fish's scales with a rubber-stamped or sponge-printed design. Or glue a sequin or small piece of paper to each scale. Glue all four cutouts together to make one long fish. When each child has constructed his fish, have him read and illustrate each of the programmed boxes. Help each youngster accordion-fold his book. These big foldout fish books are too big to go unnoticed for long. Before you know it your little ones will have lots of opportunities to "read" them and explain how they were made.

The One That Got Away

Use the fish patterns (pages 9 and 12), along with a long strip of bulletin-board paper, to create a really lengthy format for your youngsters' written expression. With your little ones, brainstorm words that they might use to describe a big, long, colorful fish. Write each suggestion on a fish-shaped word card. Cut out copies of the fish front and tail patterns (pages 9 and 12) and glue them to a strip of six-inch-wide bulletin-board paper. Begin the fish tale by writing "The fish was..." on the left end of the strip. Include the adjectives your youngsters suggested as you write one long descriptive sentence. For each word, use a color, size, and style of printing to reinforce its meaning. Post this fabulous fish tidbit, and others similar to it, on a wall. Can't you almost hear some child say, "If you think that's something, you should see the one that got away"?

A Fishbowl World

Adapt a traditional waxed-paper art technique to create see-through fishbowls full of underwater color. To begin, cut out two construction-paper fishbowls similar to the one shown. Stack the cutouts, fold them in half, and cut a semicircle from the middle so that two fishbowl-shaped frames remain when the paper is unfolded. Draw and cut out a fish shape. Fold an 11 1/2" x 15" sheet of waxed paper in half. Unfold the waxed paper. Scatter crayon shavings in a small area near the fold. Arrange some cellophane grass or tissue-paper strips so that they extend upward from the fold. Place the fish cutout about 1/2" above the crayon shavings, before refolding the paper. Momentarily center one of the fishbowl cutouts over the waxed-paper scene, to verify that the art is positioned correctly. Remove the fishbowl and place the waxed-paper scene between newspaper sheets. Quickly iron the entire waxed-paper surface with a warm iron (low setting). Spread glue on one side of each fishbowl cutout. Sandwich the waxed-paper art between the cutouts, and trim away the excess waxed paper. Tape students' completed fishbowls to a window or suspend them from the ceiling on strings.

Flashy Fish

These fantasy fish look "mah-velous" on a bright blue bulletin-board sea. To make a fish, draw or trace a large basic fish shape onto tagboard. Select two shades of the same color of tissue paper; then cut the paper into small squares. Using a large paintbrush and white glue thinned with water, coat the fish with glue. Place one tissue-paper square at a time within the fish-shaped outline, allowing the squares to overlap. Continue to add squares and glue (if necessary) until the entire cutout is covered. Coat the project with a final layer of glue. Allow the glue to dry completely, before cutting along the outline. To create the fish's tail, staple several one-inch-wide strips of tissue paper to the tail area of the cutout. Staple shorter strips to the cutout to create fins. For the fish's eye, glue on a gold foil circle or a sequin. When mounting the fish on a bulletin board, staple the strips of paper that form the tail and fins so that they are not flush with the board's surface. The flashy three-dimensional effect of these fish is sure to lure more than a few fishing enthusiasts to take a closer look.

Fish Food

The catch-of-the-day is this fish-shaped sandwich. Have your young chefs cut fish shapes from slices of wheat bread. Then obtain their assistance in making a bowl of tuna salad. Ask each child to spread a slice of fish-shaped bread with tuna salad. To complete the fish sandwich, have him add a slice of a pimento-filled green olive for the fish's eye. This treat will go well with a few small, fish-shaped pretzels.

Souvenirs Of A Splashy Unit

This fish unit souvenir will fit your students to a *T*. Ask each youngster to bring to school an undecorated, prewashed T-shirt. (Have a few spare shirts on hand for those who are unable to bring their own shirts.) Cut a sponge into a fish shape. Slide a piece of cardboard inside a shirt to prevent bleed through and to provide a firm surface for printing. In a shallow container, mix fabric or acrylic paint with textile medium. Have each child in turn press the fish-shaped sponge into the paint, onto a scrap-paper blotter, then onto his shirt to create several fish designs. Encourage students to embellish their fish designs as desired using additional fabric paints. Allow the shirts to dry before following the paint manufacturer's directions for permanently setting the paint.

Sizing Up The School

Use a school of six variously sized felt fish for lots of flannelboard fun. Have student volunteers place the fish one-by-one on a flannelboard, working from smallest to largest as you recite the following rhyme together:

That's About The Size Of It

Once there was a teeny fish
A-swimmin' in the sea.
Said the teeny fish,
"Oh, how I wish,
To see a fish bigger than me!"

Repeat the poem four more times, replacing the word teeny *with each of these words in turn:* little, average, big, *and* huge. *Then read the final verse which follows.*

Once there was a giant fish
A-swimmin' in the sea.
Said the giant fish,
"There are no fish
As big or as gorgeous as me!"
by Lucia Kemp Henry

Literature List

Swimmy
Written & Illustrated by Leo Lionni
Published by Pantheon

The Rainbow Fish
Written & Illustrated by Marcus Pfister
Translated by J. Alison James
Published by North-South Books

Fish Eyes: A Book You Can Count On
Written & Illustrated by Lois Ehlert
Published by Harcourt Brace Jovanovich, Publishers

Big Al
Written by Andrew Clements
Illustrated by Yoshi
Published by Picture Book Studio

Fish Puppet Patterns

Use with "A School Of Swimmers" and "A Fishy Tune" on page 4, and "Five Funny Fish" on page 5.

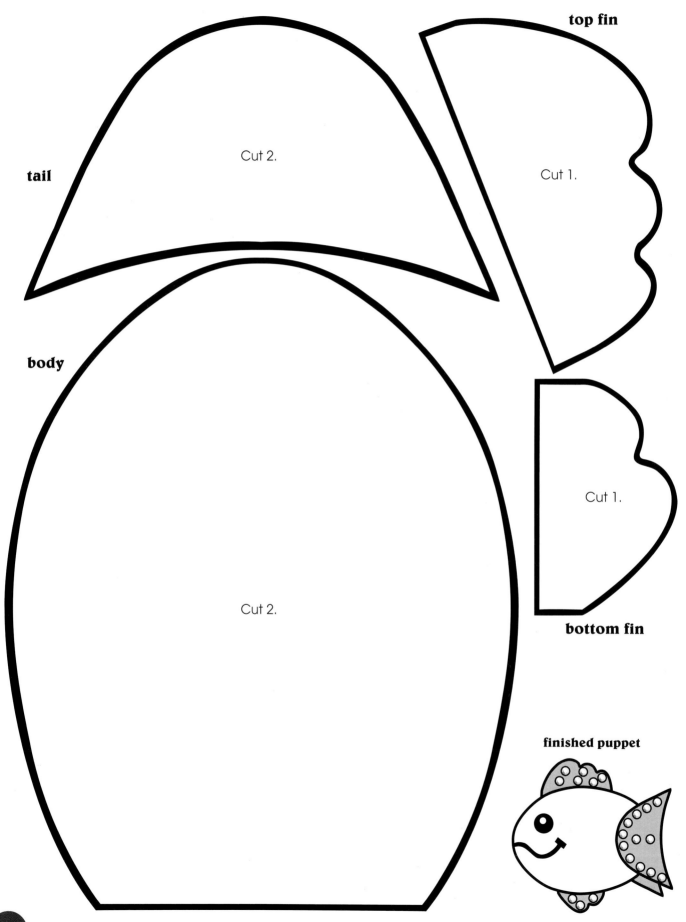

tail

top fin

Cut 2.

Cut 1.

body

Cut 2.

Cut 1.

bottom fin

finished puppet

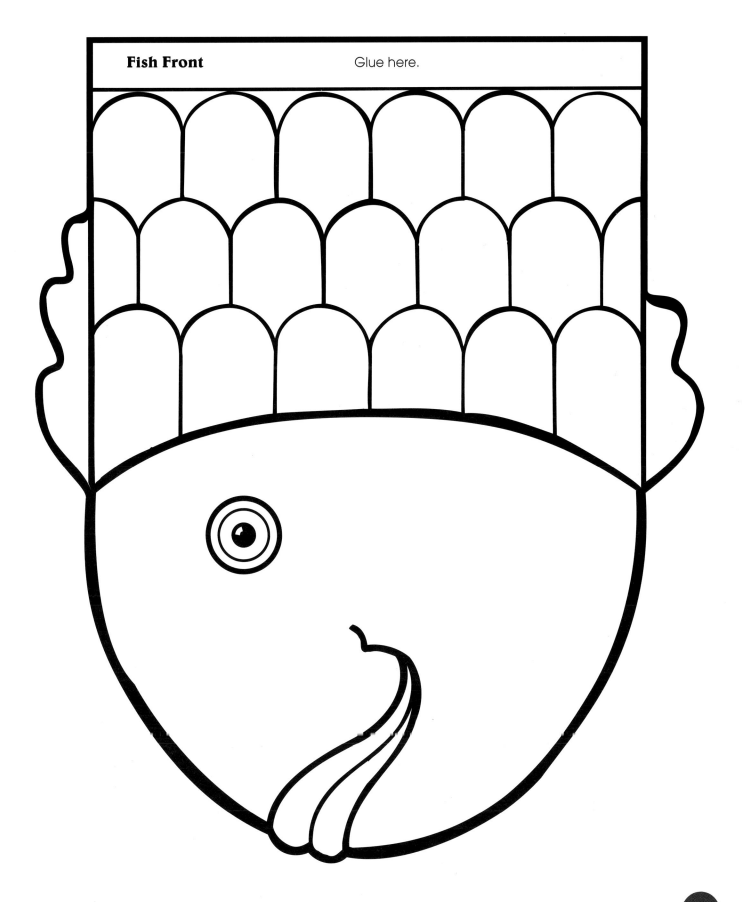

Fish Front   Glue here.

Pattern

Use with "A Foldout With Fins" on page 5.

Page 1   Glue here.

Yellow fish.

Blue fish.

One fish.

Two fish.

Page 2   Glue here.

Big fish.

Teeny fish.

Funny fish.

Meanie fish.

Fish Tail Pattern
Use with "A Foldout With Fins" and "The One That Got Away" on page 5.

©The Education Center, Inc.

Undersea Surprises

A world of new and exciting discoveries awaits your little oceanographers
as they uncover the mysteries of the sea.

ideas by Phyllis Kerley—Gr. K, Louisburg, NC, and Lori Bruce

A Great Catch

Transform your block center into a sea of adventure. Create a sea by spreading a blue sheet over the floor of the block area. Then add several mock fishing poles. To make a mock fishing pole, tape a magnet to one end of a length of string; then tape or tie the other end to a bamboo pole or dowel. Using construction paper, duplicate several copies of each of the sea creatures on pages 16 through 21. Cut them out, tape a paper clip to the back of each one, and scatter them atop the sheet. Have your crew construct fishing boats from blocks, then set sail to "catch" sea creatures with the mock fishing poles. Add a few seashells and fishing nets to the center for a wave of creative exploration.

A Taste Of The Sea

Youngsters can get a taste of the sea when you set up your own version of a seafood restaurant in your housekeeping center. Arrange and decorate tables and chairs to resemble those in a restaurant. Have youngsters create menus by gluing pictures of various types of seafood atop large sheets of construction paper that have been folded in half. Collect empty frozen seafood boxes and clean, empty oyster and clam shells to stock the "galley." "May I take your order, please?"

Kerley's
Taste
of the
Sea

Sizing Up Sea Life

Youngsters will want to get in the swim of things with the terrific visual discrimination and seriation skills at this manipulative center. Using various colors of construction paper, duplicate copies of the sea creatures on pages 16 through 21. Then use a copier to reduce each pattern to a smaller size before duplicating another set of creatures onto construction paper. Repeat this procedure one more time to produce an even-smaller-size set of sea creatures. Cut out the creatures and laminate them for durability. Store them in a fishbowl or large Ziploc® bag. To use this center, a youngster sorts the creatures by species, color, or size. As a variation, each set of creatures can be arranged in order from smallest to largest.

Fish Tales

Make a splash with this student-created booklet of fish tales. After masking the facial features of the fish pattern on page 21, duplicate a copy for each youngster. Have each youngster cut out his copy and draw a picture of the sea creature he would most like to have as a pet on it. Then have him write or dictate a sentence or two about his unusual pet. To make covers for the booklet, trace the outline of the fish shape onto two sheets of construction paper. Cut out both covers and have youngsters decorate them as desired. Staple youngsters' completed pages between the construction paper covers. Select additional topics and/or shapes to create an entire school of fish tales for your classroom library.

I would keep an octopus in my bathtub.
Sam

Mural Magic

Create your own

Ocean Floor

To complete a background for the mural, spread a long piece of blue bulletin-board paper on the floor. Have youngsters paint the bottom fourth of the paper with thinned white glue. Have them sprinkle sand atop the glue. After the glue has dried, shake off the excess sand and glue on small seashells if desired.

Seaweed And Coral

Add a little pizzazz to your background with lifelike plants and coral reefs. Dip pasta shapes in green tempera paint; then remove them and spread them out to dry atop several layers of paper toweling. When dry, glue the dyed pasta shapes on the mural to resemble various sea plants. Fold sheets of pink and purple construction paper or tissue paper in half, and tear irregular shapes from them. Unfold the paper; then glue the resulting shapes atop the mural to resemble a coral reef. Staple the completed background to a bulletin board.

Extraordinary Octopuses

These tentacled creations are anything but ordinary! Using green construction paper, duplicate a copy of the pattern on page 19 for each child. To make an extraordinary octopus, cut out the pattern along the bold outline. Fill a spray bottle with a light color of thinned tempera paint. For a mottled effect, lightly spray the paint over the entire cutout. Glue round Styrofoam® packing circles along one side of each tentacle. To complete the project, glue on a pair of marble eyes and a length of yarn for a mouth. An outburst of oceanographic interest is sure to follow these extraordinary creatures.

Sensational Sea Horses

Prepare to be stampeded with interested oceanographers when you create these special sea horses. Using orange construction paper, duplicate a copy of the pattern on page 18 for each child. To make a sensational sea horse, cut out the pattern along the bold outline. Then tear thumb-size pieces of brown grocery bags and glue them atop the cutout. Glue on a button for an eye. Accordion fold a one-foot length of orange crepe-paper streamer. Unfold it and glue it along the spine and tail of the cutout. Then cut ten strips from a four-inch length of the orange streamer. To complete the sea horse, twist the strips together and glue them to the back of the cutout to resemble a dorsal fin.

Cereal-studded Starfish

Create star-quality starfish with Cheerios®. Using red construction paper, duplicate a copy of the pattern on page 16 for each child. To make a cereal-studded starfish, cut out the pattern along the bold outline. Glue aquarium rocks atop the cutout for eyes and a mouth if desired. Then glue Cheerios® atop the remaining areas of the cutout. "Neat-O!"

jennifer tipton

magical undersea mural.

Sea Creatures

Once the ocean floor, seaweed, and coral are in place, bring your mural alive with student-made sea creatures. Duplicate copies of the sea creatures on pages 16 through 21. Have each youngster select his favorite creature, then cut it out and paint or color it before gluing it atop the mural. Or use some or all of the suggestions below to create an artsy, nonrealistic version of each sea creature. After attaching the sea creatures to the mural, have students create a graph to represent its underwater population.

Jiggling Jellyfish

Jiggling jellyfish jazz up any undersea display. Using purple construction paper, duplicate a copy of the pattern on page 17 for each child. To make a jiggling jellyfish, cut out the pattern along the bold outline. Use a hole punch to punch six holes as indicated on the pattern. Sponge paint the entire cutout using white shoe polish in a bottle with a sponge-tip applicator. To create arms, twist two, two-foot lengths of plastic wrap. Tape the center of each arm to the bottom of the cutout. For tentacles, cut six, three-foot lengths of pink curling ribbon. Fold a length in half, creating a loop. Working from back to front, insert the loop through a hole in the cutout; then pull the loose ends up through the loop. Gently pull the ends to tighten. Attach each of the remaining ribbons in the same way, before curling them. Glue on buttons for eyes and a row of sequins for a mouth if desired. These jiggly creatures are sure to create a wave of excitement.

Fabulous Fish

Create schools of colorful fish with this collage technique. Using yellow construction paper, duplicate one copy of the pattern on page 21 for each child. To make a fabulous fish, cut out the pattern along the bold outline. Using pinking shears, cut strips of aluminum foil, construction paper, and ribbon. Glue the strips atop the cutout along with lengths of rickrack and yarn to create a collage of texture and color. Drizzle trails of glue atop the cutout; then sprinkle with glitter for a dazzling effect. Glue on a pom-pom for an eye. These beautiful creations are sure to captivate young undersea explorers.

Snappy Crabs

Motivate youngsters to explore the ocean depths with these clever crabs. Using pink construction paper, duplicate a copy of the pattern on page 20 for each child. To make a snappy crab, cut out the pattern along the bold outline. Place a paper towel which has been folded into fourths into a Styrofoam® meat tray. Soak the paper towel with blue tempera paint. Then repeatedly press a thumb into the paint and onto the cutout until the entire shell is covered with thumbprints. Cut two sections from an egg carton. Glue one side of each section atop the front claws to resemble pincers. Glue on two pom-pom eyes and a length of yarn for a mouth. To make antennae, fold a pipe cleaner into a *v* shape. To complete the project, curl each end of the pipe cleaner; then tape it onto the cutout just above the pom-pom eyes.

Starfish Pattern

Use with "A Great Catch" and "Sizing Up Sea Life" on page 13, "Cereal-studded Starfish" on page 14, and "Sea Creatures" on page 15.

Jellyfish Pattern
Use with "A Great Catch" and
"Sizing Up Sea Life" on page 13
and "Sea Creatures" and "Jiggling Jellyfish" on page 15.

Sea Horse Pattern

Use with "A Great Catch" and "Sizing Up Sea Life" on page 13, "Sensational Sea Horses" on page 14, and "Sea Creatures" on page 15.

Use with "A Great Catch" and "Sizing Up Sea Life" on page 13, "Extraordinary Octopuses" on page 14, and "Sea Creatures" on page 15.

Crab Pattern

Use with "A Great Catch" and "Sizing Up Sea Life" on page 13 and "Snappy Crabs" and "Sea Creatures" on page 15.

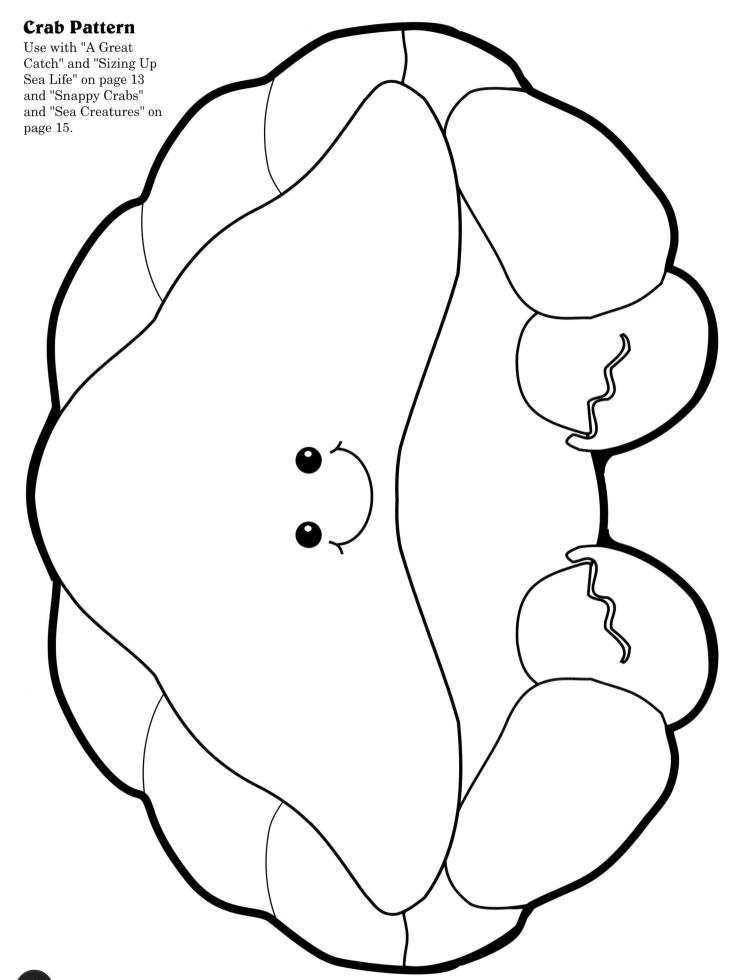

Fish Pattern
Use with "A Great Catch," "Sizing Up Sea Life," and "Fish Tales" on page 13 and "Fabulous Fish" and "Sea Creatures" on page 15.

The Wonder Of Whales

The largest of them all is larger than the biggest dinosaur ever was. The smallest is about the size of a man. They are graceful in the water and awe-inspiring when they leap from it. These magnificent mammals are certain to spark your little ones' curiosity and creativity. Dive in!

by Lucia Kemp Henry

What Is A Whale?

Introduce your youngsters to the world of whales by having them imitate your actions as you say this rhyme together.

A whale is not as small as us.   *Shake head and finger.*
Most whales are bigger than a bus!   *Stretch arms out wide.*

A whale is not like a fish in the sea. *Shake head and finger.*
A whale breathes air like you and me.   *Take a deep breath.*

A whale can't walk upon the ground.   *Shake head and finger.*
A whale must swim to get around.   *Make swimming motions.*

A whale is a mammal just like me.   *Nod head and point to self.*
But its home is in the deep blue sea!   *Make wave motions with hand.*

By Lucia Kemp Henry

Underwater Wonders

Spark discussions about whales by sharing some factual information with your youngsters. Use picture books and reference books as visual aids. At the conclusion of this discussion, have each youngster identify the whale fact that he found most interesting. Write as he dictates what he has learned about whales. Then have him illustrate his dictation.

- Whales are mammals—not fish.
- Whales breathe air.
- The biggest whale, the blue whale, can weigh as much as 32 elephants.
- Some whales have teeth. They catch fish with their teeth. Orcas, sperm whales, belugas, and dolphins are toothed whales.
- Some whales' mouths have sievelike *baleen*. Baleen are used to filter tiny animals called *plankton* from the seawater. Blue, humpback, right, and gray whales are baleen whales.
- The *blowholes* (nostrils) of whales are on the tops of their heads.
- Whales' tails are called *flukes*.
- Paddlelike limbs on the sides of whales are called *flippers*. The bones in flippers of toothed whales look like finger bones.
- A fin is located on the back of most kinds of whales.
- Whales are covered with skin—not scales.

The Expedition

Observant youngsters will be the first to spy whale cutouts during this classroom whale-watching expedition. To prepare for this activity, explain to your students that they will be whale watching during the following day, and ask that they bring plastic sunglasses to cut down on glare. (Have several extra pairs of sunglasses on hand for those who forget.) Duplicate and cut out construction-paper copies of the whales on pages 27–31. (Make a few more whales than you have students.) Before students arrive the following morning, tuck each whale cutout into a different hiding place so that the turned-up tail of the whale is all that can be seen.

When you are ready to begin the day with you students, have them don their sunglasses and wander about the classroom "ocean" looking for whales. Ask each student to collect only one whale. When everyone has one, have the students with matching whales group together. Then use reference books to briefly discuss each type of whale that the children have found. A wonderful way to end this exercise would be to read aloud the book *I Wonder If I'll See A Whale* by Frances Ward Weller.

adapted from an idea by Ruthann Hardy Szanati
Alpha, NJ

Pam Crane

Whale Watcher's Guide

Look, Dad, we've been studying about whales! Your youngsters are certain to be excited about their whale studies when you use this whale identification booklet. For each student, duplicate a copy of the cover and each booklet page (pages 26–31) on white construction paper. Collate the pages and bind each booklet using staples or plastic rings. Have each youngster label the cover of his booklet with his name. Then, over the course of several days, lead students in discussing each featured whale before having youngsters color its page. To add more interest, ocean animal stickers may be added to stapled booklets and dyed ocean animal-shaped pasta may be glued to ring-bound booklets.

The whales in the booklet are not drawn to scale. To give youngsters an idea of how the sizes of whales compare, encourage them to examine the pictures in a whale reference book such as *Whales Zoobooks* by John Bonnett Wexo.

Artistic Display

Get your entire crew involved in this artistic whale display. Staple a length of light blue bulletin-board paper across the top of a bulletin board. Color and cut out an enlargement of the boat-and-boy design (page 26). Staple the boat to the left side of the board, about a third of the way down. Cut blue bulletin-board paper the same length as the first piece, and lay it on a newspaper-covered area. Thin blue, green, and white tempera paint with water. Pour each color of thinned paint into a different spray bottle. Have youngsters take turns spraying paint onto the paper, and allow the paint to dry. Measure the minimum depth for the bulletin board's water; then use this measurement to cut one long edge of the spray-painted paper into "waves." Attach the paper to the board.

Finish the display with a splash. Have students fingerpaint using gray or black paint and large sheets of paper. Trace an enlarged whale outline (page 25) onto the back of each dried paper. Or have each student draw a whale outline freehand. Have students cut out their whales and attach wiggle eyes to the painted sides before mounting them on the board.

Dolphin Dance

One of the things that makes dolphins so fascinating is their ability to leap and dance in plain view. Have your little ones imitate these graceful cetaceans as they move to classical music. One readily available recording is from Beethoven's Symphony No. 6 (*Pastoral*). Play the third movement, Allegro ("Jolly Gathering Of Country Folk"), which has a rolling beat similar to the rhythm of a playful dolphin. Inspired by the music, invite your dolphin dancers to take the plunge and move like dolphins do in their ocean playground (classroom). Explain that dolphins are graceful and smart, so they avoid crashing into other dolphins.

To conclude the activity, lower the volume of the music and ask your dolphin dancers to "swim" in a circle and join "flippers." Have students circle slowly as you lower the music. Then have them lie down on the floor, with their "flukes" (feet) pointing into the circle.

Whale Counting Rhyme

Dive into this flannelboard activity with whales you can count on. Duplicate the whale patterns (page 25) onto blue tagboard or construction paper. Cut out the whales and back the cutouts with felt strips. Recite the counting rhyme, placing whales on a flannelboard as indicated. When all ten whales are on the flannelboard, give volunteers several opportunities to count them.

Counting Little Whales

One little whale
Two little whales
I can see three blue little whales.

Four little whales
Five little whales
I can see six live little whales.

Seven little whales
Eight little whales
I can see nine great little whales.

Ten little whales
Ten little whales
I can count all ten little whales!

Paper Bag Whales

Your little ones can make some cute cetaceans using paper bags and construction paper scraps. To make a whale, place an unopened, brown lunch bag on a table. Near the top of the bag, place and trace the fluke pattern (page 32). Remove the pattern and cut along the traced lines through all thicknesses. For the blowhole, cut a small X in the bag. Open the bag, and stuff it lightly (about 3/4 of the way full) with tissue or newspaper. Staple the fluke ends closed; then staple along the sides of the fluke. Staple the remaining openings as shown. Use markers to draw a mouth and eyes. Roll up a 4 1/2" x 12" piece of blue construction paper to form a cylinder that is 4 1/2 inches tall. Glue or tape the paper so it can't unroll. Snip one end of the cylinder several times, cutting only about halfway down. Curl the fringed ends to resemble a waterspout before inserting the spout into the blowhole. Cut two flippers (patterns on page 32) from paper scraps and glue them to the whale's sides.

Whales In A Bottle

Whether your youngsters assist you in making one of these whale tanks or they each make individual ones to keep, this project is going to make a big splash. Remove the black plastic bottom from a two-liter soft-drink bottle for this activity. Fill the bottle about one-quarter full of water. Tint the water with food coloring and add a drop of liquid detergent. Drop in a few pieces of aquarium gravel. For whales, inflate two small blue balloons, release most of the air, and tie the ends closed. Push the balloons into the bottle and screw the cap on tightly. Children will enjoy tilting these bottles back and forth to watch their whales swim.

Ruthann Hardy Szanati
Alpha, NJ

Splashin' Around

Most kinds of whales travel together in groups called *pods*. Dive into these movement activities with your classroom pod of whale imitators.

- Group students into pairs and have each pair lie on the floor with "flukes" (feet) touching. Have each pair of fluke-connected students attempt to roll across the floor without breaking the fluke connection.
- Group students into pairs and give each pair a ball. Ask each pair to work cooperatively to hold a ball between their backs. Once this is accomplished, have them try holding the ball between their foreheads, chests, and stomachs.
- Designate four students to be a whale pod. Have three of the whales leave the room while the fourth hides. When the pod returns to find their missing member, they must stay together holding hands while looking for the missing whale. The pod forms a circle around the hiding member when he is found. Play continues in this manner with new groups of students taking turns. Add another element of fun by playing Raffi's "Baby Beluga" as each pod searches.
- Form one large whale pod in this whale pod roundup. Set the mood by playing music, if desired. To begin have each youngster "swim" slowly around the room. Call out, "Whales, find a friend." At this signal, each youngster pairs up with another. When this is done, pairs of youngsters swim around the room together. Then call out, "Whales, find some friends!" Each whale pair joins with another pair and resumes swimming. Continue until one large pod is formed.

Patterns
Use with "Whale Counting Rhyme" on page 23.
Enlarge to use with "Artistic Display" on page 23.

©The Education Center, Inc.

©The Education Center, Inc.

©The Education Center, Inc.

©The Education Center, Inc.

Whale Watcher's Guide

Note To Teacher: Use with "Whale Watcher's Guide" on page 23. Enlarge to use with "Artistic Display" on page 23.

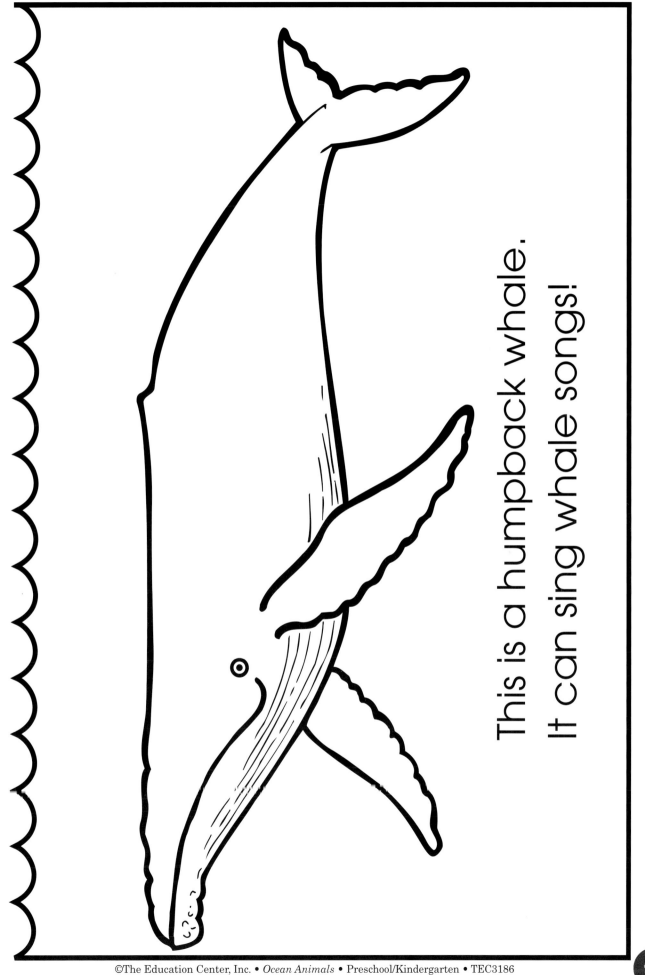

This is a humpback whale.
It can sing whale songs!

Note To Teacher: Use with "The Expedition" on page 22 and "Whale Watcher's Guide" on page 23.

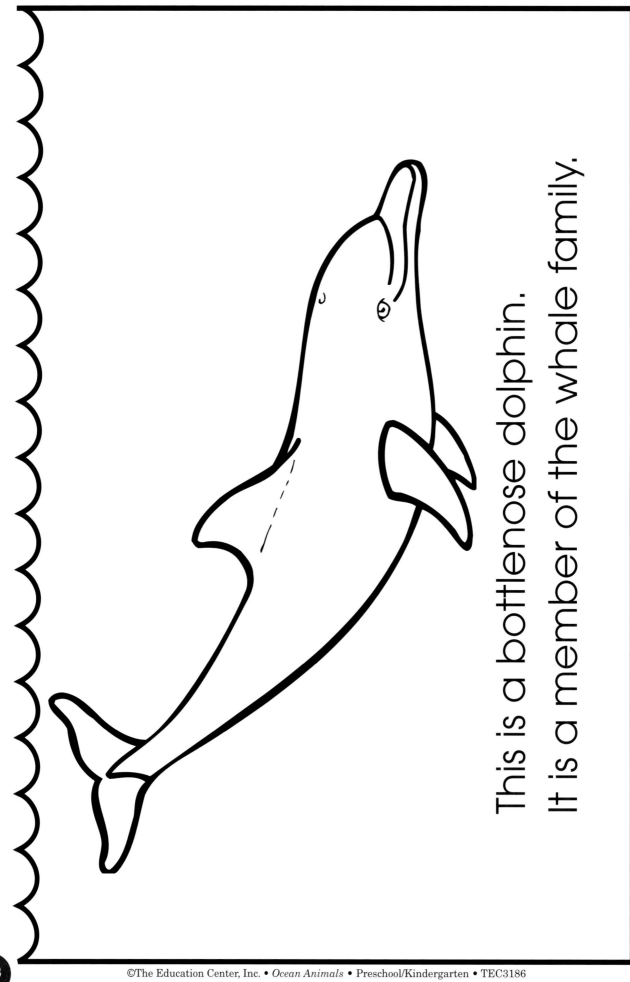

This is a bottlenose dolphin.
It is a member of the whale family.

Note To Teacher: Use with "The Expedition" on page 22 and "Whale Watcher's Guide" on page 23.

This is an orca whale.
It is black and white.

Note To Teacher: Use with "The Expedition" on page 22 and "Whale Watcher's Guide" on page 23.

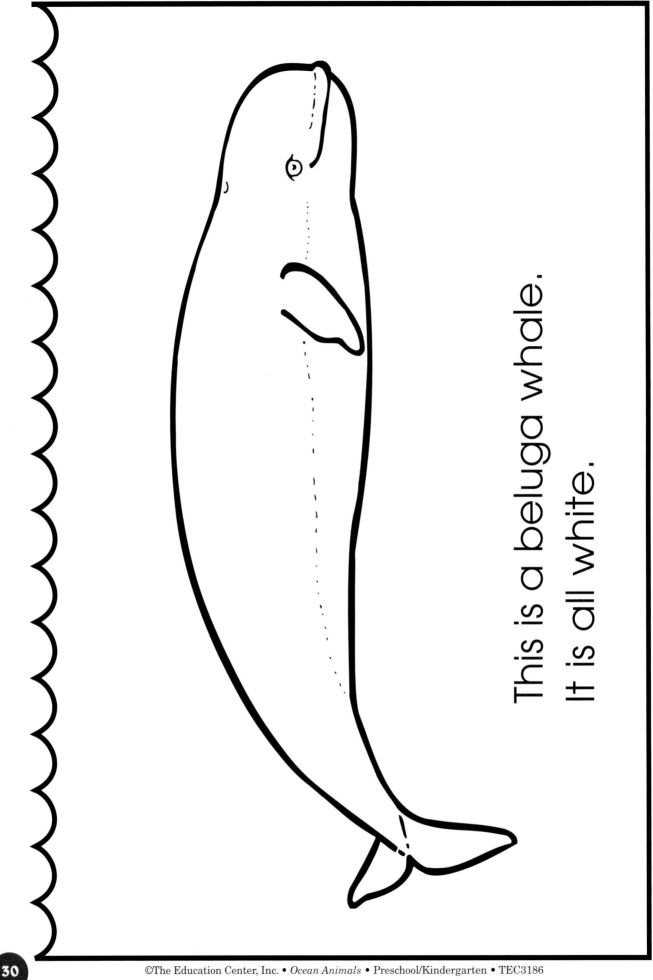

This is a beluga whale.
It is all white.

Note To Teacher: Use with "The Expedition" on page 22 and "Whale Watcher's Guide" on page 23.

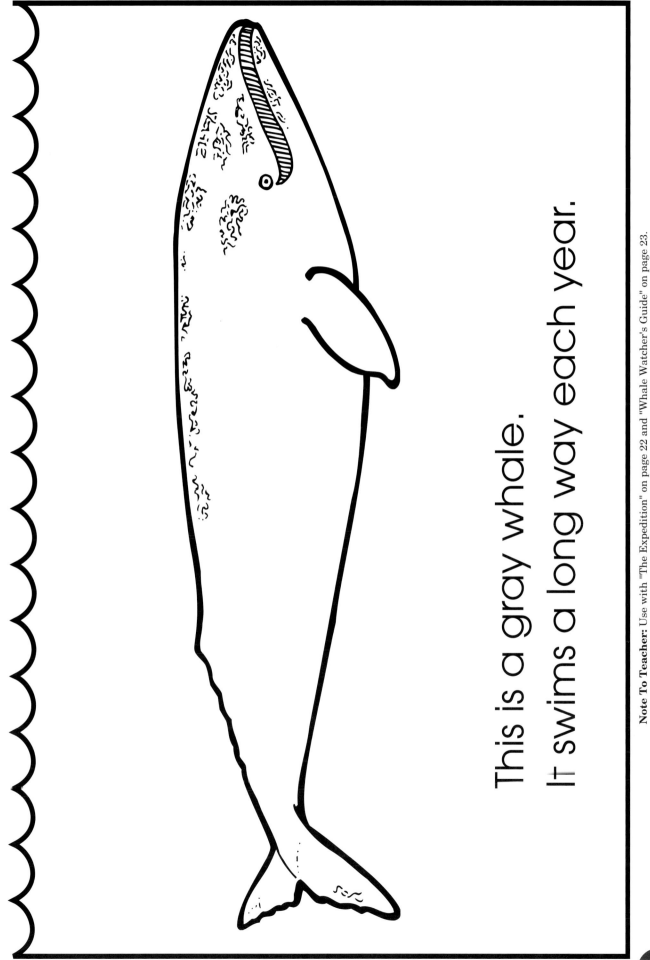

This is a gray whale.
It swims a long way each year.

Note To Teacher: Use with "The Expedition" on page 22 and "Whale Watcher's Guide" on page 23.

©The Education Center, Inc. • *Ocean Animals* • Preschool/Kindergarten • TEC3186

31

Pattern

Use with "Paper Bag Whales" on page 24.

completed project

flippers

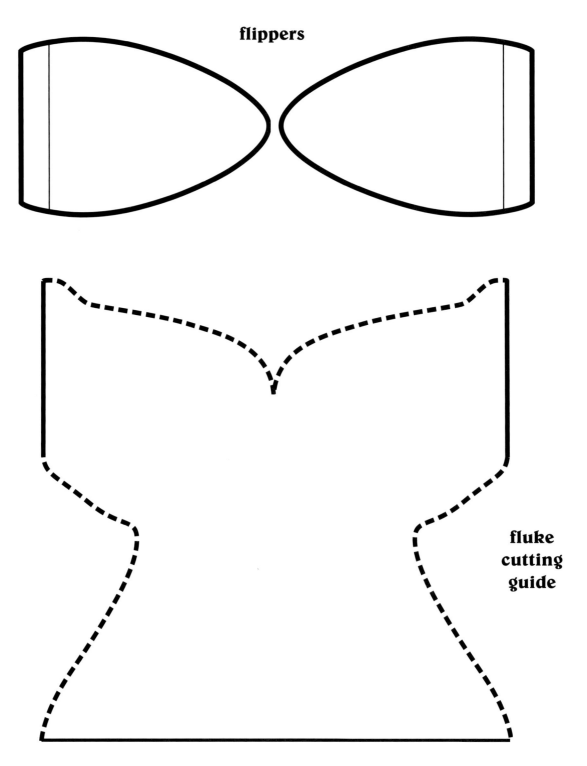

fluke
cutting
guide

More Ideas To Dive Into

Sweet Starfish

Students will create star-quality starfish with this sweet painting technique. Combine sugar and several drops of food coloring with enough water to create a thick but paintable mixture. Use crayons to add features to a construction-paper starfish. Then paint the sugar mixture onto the starfish or spread the mixture on with your fingers. When the sugar mixture is dry, add these sweet starfish to a sand-and-surf display.

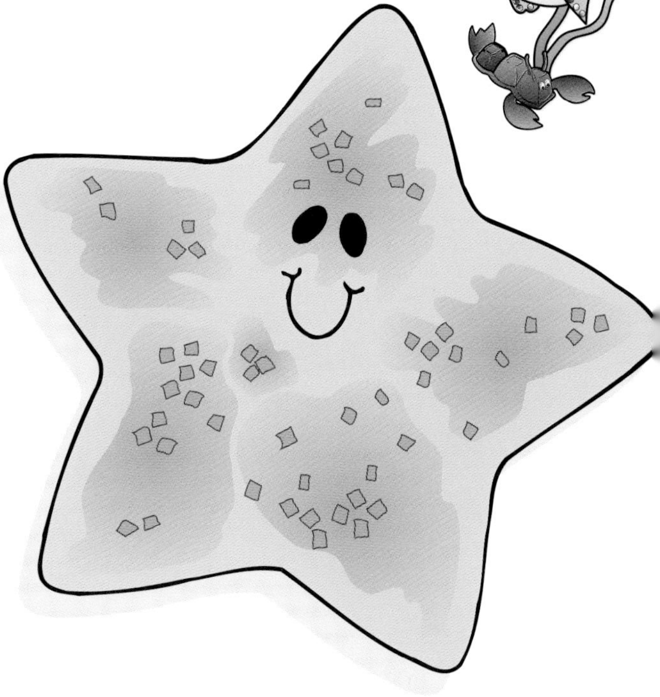

Joannie Netzler—Three-Year-Olds
A Special Place
San Jose, CA

Five Little Fishes

Thinking about teasing Mr. Shark? Be careful!
He eats one more fish with each consecutive verse of this rhyme!

[Five] little fishes,

Swimming in the sea.

Teasing Mr. Shark,

"You can't catch me!"

Along comes Mr. Shark,

As quiet as can be...

Snap!

[Four] little fishes,

Swimming in the sea.

—*Andrea Esposito, Brooklyn, NY*

Flashy Fish

Splish, splash! These flashy fish will swim by just in time to create a fantastic display. To create a one-of-a-kind fish, glue oval-shaped tissue paper and foil pieces onto a white construction-paper fish shape. Attach a black dot sticker to resemble an eye. Punch a hole near the mouth of the fish. To display, suspend a length of rope from your ceiling; then attach the fish to the rope by sliding one end of an opened paper clip through the rope and the other end through the fish's mouth. Wow—what a catch!

Gail Moody—Preschool
Atascadero Parent Education Preschool
Atascadero, CA

The Deep Blue Sea

Youngsters will be entranced by the sparkling blue "ocean" waters in these tiny kid-made aquariums. To make an aquarium, decorate the outside of a clean, empty baby-food jar with fish stickers. Put a few small shells inside. Nearly fill the jar with water. To the water, add a drop or two of food coloring and some blue glitter. Use a hot glue gun to seal the lid of each youngster's jar and prevent leaking. Who could resist shaking these miniaquariums to watch the fishes' glittering ocean backdrop?

Nanette Singleton
Real Life Play School
Kokomo, IN

May I Keep Them?

From a distance these bagged fish could pass for the real thing. Not only will your youngsters have a ball making them, but they'll also delight in the reactions of others. To make a bag of fish, turn an airtight, clear, plastic bag inside out. Cut out and decorate several small, construction-paper fish. On one side of the bag, near the bottom, glue some of your fish cutouts. When these have dried, turn the bag over and glue the remaining fish to the other side. When this glue has dried, turn the bag right side out. Puff air into the bag, trapping it with a rubber band. Display these fish with a sign that says "Fish For Sale—Five Cents Each."

Carol DeKoninck—Preschool
Christian Child Care Center
Grand Ledge, MI

Edible Aquariums

Get into the swim of things with these fun-to-make edible aquariums. To make an edible aquarium, add a few drops of blue food coloring to a container of softened cream cheese. Spread some of the cream cheese mixture atop a piece of melba toast; then press on a few tiny goldfish crackers. These snack sensations are sure to make quite a splash with your youngsters!

Sherry Sentell—Gr. K
St. Alphonsus School
Ocean Springs, MS

A Rock Lobster

This under-the-sea creature will really make a splash in your classroom. To make a rock lobster, cut off a row of three cardboard egg-carton cups. Paint the sections of the carton to resemble a lobster's body. When the paint dries, color and cut out a lobster tail and two claws. Glue the claw cutouts to one end of the lobster and the tail cutout to the other end. Then attach two pipe cleaners to resemble antennae. Glue two wiggle eyes to complete the lobster. Now this is a craft your little ones can put their claws on!

Ms. Guanipa—Gr. K, Covenant School, Arlington, MA

How Many Fish Today?

9

This underwater counting board will make a big splash with little ones. Have children add construction-paper plant life and shells to a blue bulletin-board background. Title the board with foil or neon-colored letter cutouts. Then stock a center with fish-making supplies and let youngsters have at it! Mount each day's new fish on the board and count the new total together. Encourage children to predict what each day's new number will be.

Helaine Rooney—Gr. K, Georgian Forest Elementary, Silver Spring, MD

Handprint Octopus

Journey to the depths of the ocean and you'll find these awesome octopi. Using fluorescent liquid tempera paint, paint a child's palm one color and his fingers (excluding his thumb) four different colors. Have him press his hand on a sheet of black construction paper with his fingers pointed toward a lower corner of the paper. Then have him press just his fingers under the palm print toward the other lower corner to resemble the remaining four arms of the octopus. When the paint is dry, glue two wiggle eyes to the octopus and add facial features with a marker. If desired add ocean-related stickers to the paper to create an underwater scene.

Jan Stremel—Four-Year-Olds, St. Paul Preschool, Dallas, TX

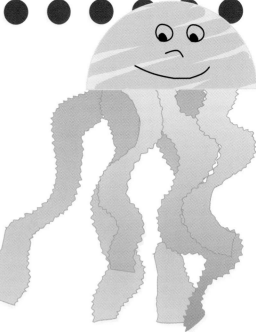

Jellyfish

Here's a school of sea critters that your youngsters will be eager to make! To make a jellyfish, paint a half of a paper plate the color or colors of your choice, and allow it to dry. Use pinking shears to cut strips of tissue paper. Then glue the tissue-paper strips to the plate so that they hang down. To complete the project, use a marker to draw facial features on the jellyfish. Mount these colorful jellyfish on a wall or bulletin board for a special display.

Linda Anne Lopienski
Asheboro, NC

Twist-Off Tops

During your study of the ocean, invite little ones to create sea scenes for these clever crustaceans! Recycle the twist-off tops from Kool-Aid® squeeze bottles. The tops resemble lobsters and are easy for children to glue onto their drawings. Collect the twist-off tops in various colors to use for patterning, sorting, and other math activities too.

Susan Turpin—Pre-K
Pied Piper Kindergarten
Jacksonville, FL

Jell-O® Fish Bags

Here's a fun fishy snack your youngsters are sure to enjoy! Spoon several scoops of prepared blue Jell-O® into a resealable plastic bag. Add a few Gummy fish candies; then seal the bag securely. Children can make their fish swim around by squishing them through the plastic bags. Then pass out the spoons for a tasty snack!

Karen Smith—Grs. K–1

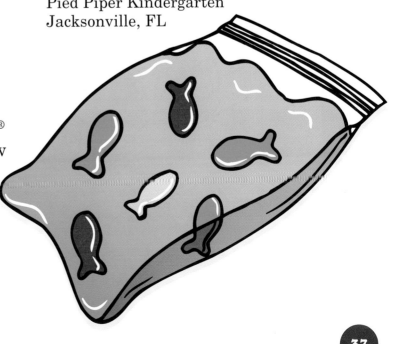

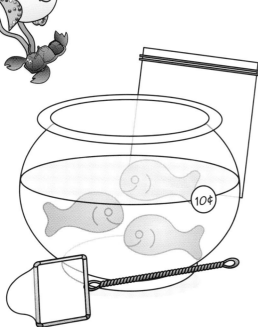

Fish-Shop Play

Setting up a fish shop in your dramatic-play area is great fun—not to mention good practice in math, fine-motor, and social skills. Fill several different fishbowls with water; then add colorful plastic fish to each bowl. Label each bowl with a price; then arrange the bowls in your dramatic-play area along with a small fishnet, plastic bags, and some coins. (Also provide some extra coins for the shoppers!) Encourage children to take turns being the shop clerk and the customers.

Karen Smith—Grs. K–1

Whale Of A Tail

You can reinforce a whole pod of different skills with this whale center. To make the center, cut out whale shapes from construction paper. Program each head with the skill of your choice, such as a numeral, a beginning-consonant picture, or a color dot. Program the tail with the corresponding element. Then puzzle-cut each of the whales. To use this center, a child matches each whale with its corresponding tail.

Cindy Stefanick—Gr. K
Roosevelt School, Worcester, MA

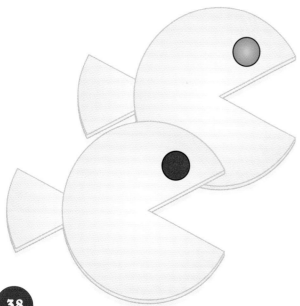

Fish Cookies

One nibble, and your youngsters will be hooked on these easy-to-make fish cookies. For each cookie, cut a circle shape from sugar-cookie dough. Cut a triangle from the circle. Attach the tip of the triangle to the opposite side of the circle. Press an M&M candy into the dough for an eye. Bake the cookies according to the sugar cookie recipe. If you made the "Jell-O® Fish Bags" described on page 37, consider serving the cookies and the gelatin together to culminate your ocean animal theme.

Alyson Rappaport and Kim Singleton—Preschool
Prodigy Day Care, Stone Mountain, GA

Reproducible Activities...

from TEACHER'S HELPER® magazine.

The Rainbow Fish

Note To The Teacher
Duplicate the book note below for each child. Have each child color and cut out his book note. Encourage students to take their book notes home and share the story's content.

Related Literature—Sea-Related Books

Swimmy
Written & Illustrated by Leo Lionni
Published by Alfred A. Knopf, Inc.

Fish Eyes: A Book You Can Count On
Written & Illustrated by Lois Ehlert
Published by Harcourt Brace Jovanovich, Publishers

Big Al
Written by Andrew Clements
Illustrated by Yoshi
Published by Picture Book Studio

Nature Hide & Seek: Oceans
Written by John Norris Wood
Illustrated by Mark Harrison
Published by Alfred A. Knopf, Inc.

Book Note

I heard the story
The Rainbow Fish
by Marcus Pfister.

Do you want to know
what happens in the story?
Ask me!

Name

Fishy Friends

Show which animals were in the story.

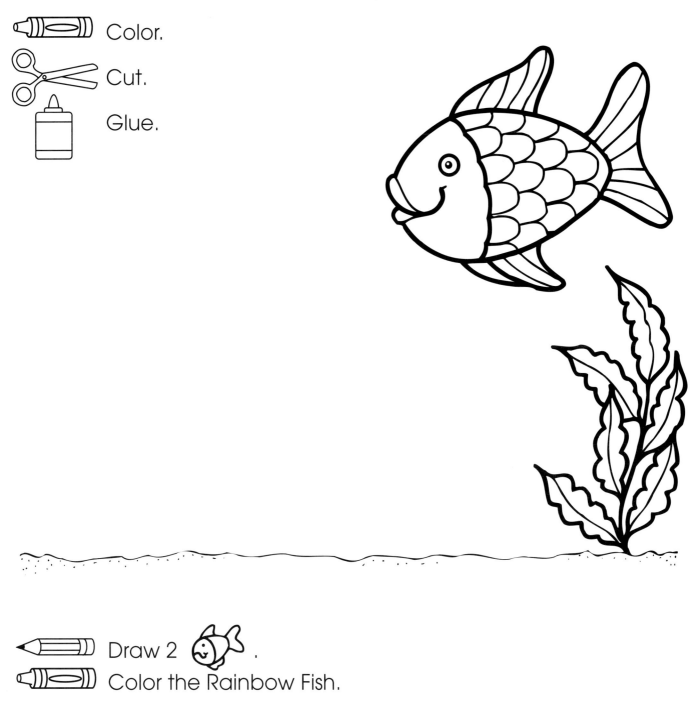

Color.

Cut.

Glue.

Draw 2 🐟 .
Color the Rainbow Fish.

©The Education Center, Inc. • *Ocean Animals* • Preschool/Kindergarten • TEC3186

Fish Feelings

When the Rainbow Fish gave away his scales, how did all the fish feel?

Cut.

Glue.

Draw scales on the fish.

Bonus Box: Draw something that you like to share with your friends on the back of your paper.

The Rainbow Fish

Finished Sample

Programmable Activity Cards

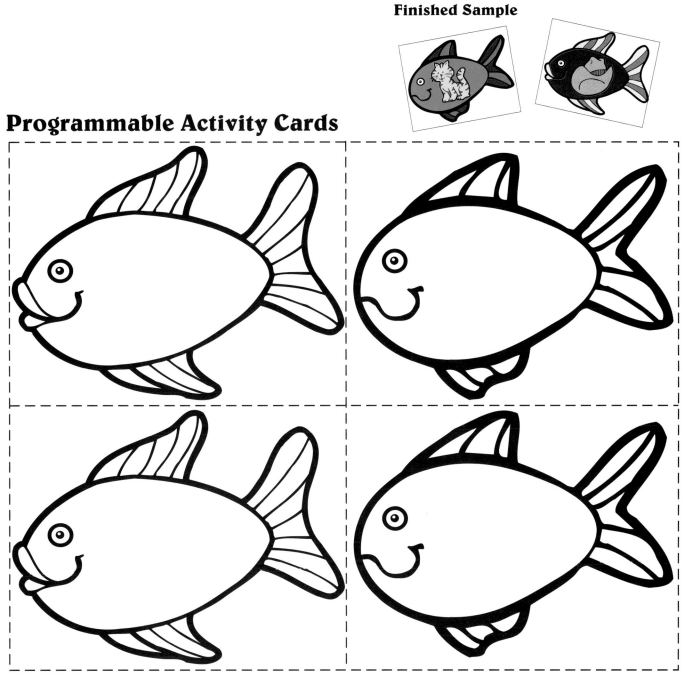

..Under-The-Sea Serenade..

How To Use Page 45

1. Duplicate the page for each child.
2. Have each child cut along the dotted lines and then glue where indicated on the gray area.
3. If desired, have youngsters write the numeral one under the first sea horse and the numeral two under the second sea horse, then continue numbering the sea horses through the tenth sea horse. Review the ordinal number for each horse.
4. Have your youngsters listen to these directions and follow them.

- *Find the second sea horse. Draw a blue hat on it.*
- *Find the fifth sea horse. Color it red.*
- *Locate the eighth sea horse on your strip. Draw purple spots on its stomach.*
- *Put your finger on the sixth sea horse. Draw a yellow circle around it.*
- *Find the tenth sea horse. Color its musical instrument green.*

- *Place your finger on the first sea horse. Draw brown sand under it.*
- *Count to the seventh sea horse. Draw blue bubbles above it.*
- *Find the ninth sea horse. Color its tail black.*
- *Put your finger on the third sea horse. Draw a yellow crown on its head.*
- *Locate the fourth sea horse. Color it orange.*

Finished Project

Listen and do. **Sea Horse Swimming Band**

44

Glue strips together here.

Sea Horse Swimming Band

Listen and do.

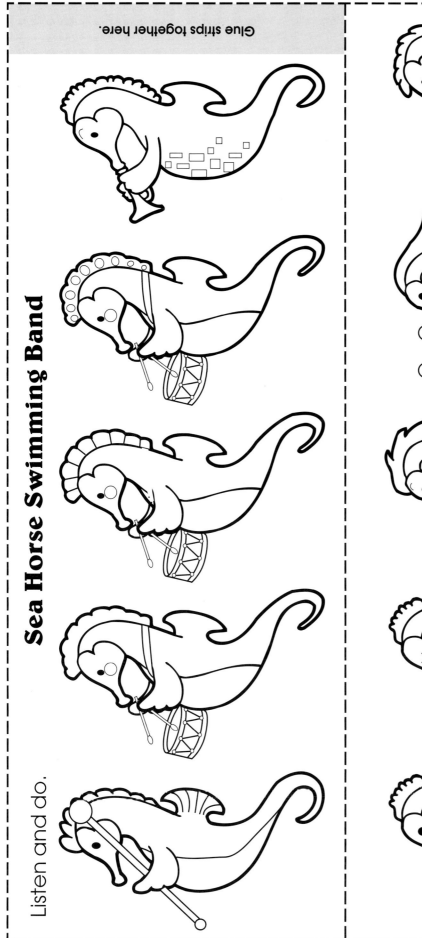

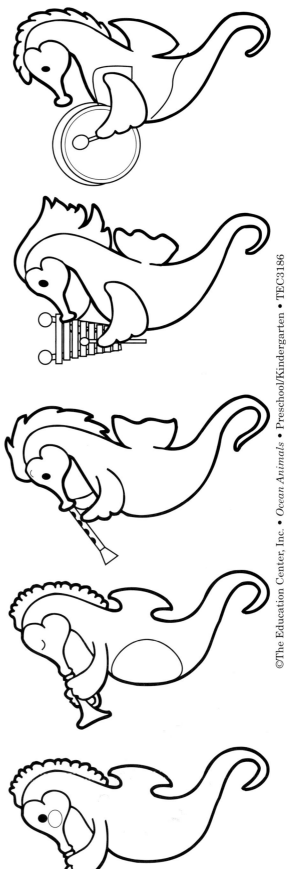

..Under-The-Sea Serenade..

How To Use Pages 46, 47, And 48

1. Duplicate a copy of pages 46, 47, 48, and two rows of the sea critter counters below for each child.
2. Have each child color the sea critter counters, then cut them apart.
3. Direct each child to use the counters to determine the sums; then glue the correct number sentences in the shaded spaces on page 47 and write the correct sums in the starfish on page 48.

Sea Critter Counters

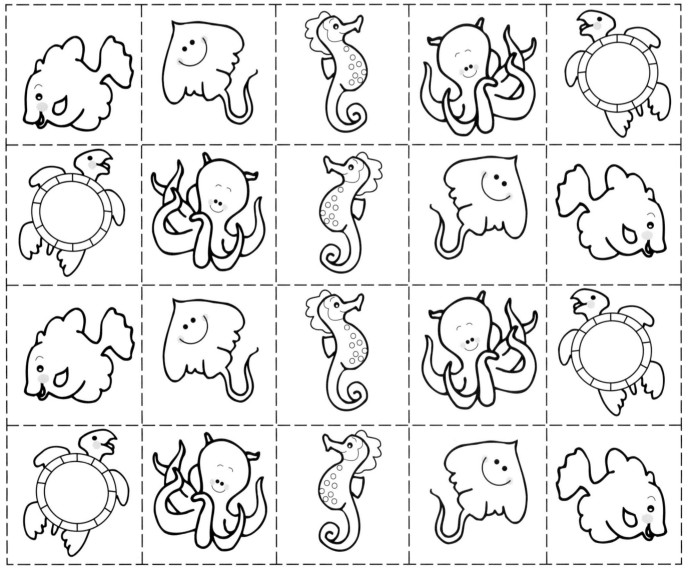

Rhythm In The Waves

Add.
Cut.
Glue.

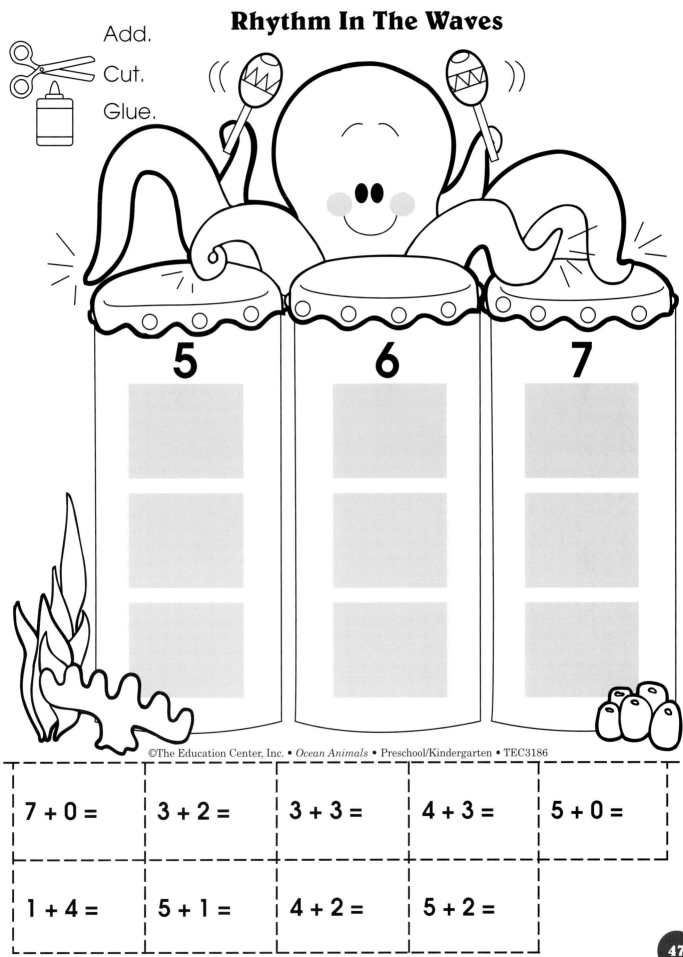

5

6

7

©The Education Center, Inc. • *Ocean Animals* • Preschool/Kindergarten • TEC3186

7 + 0 =	3 + 2 =	3 + 3 =	4 + 3 =	5 + 0 =
1 + 4 =	5 + 1 =	4 + 2 =	5 + 2 =	

Name _____

Pacific Pipers

Add.
Write the answer.

$2 + 6 =$

$5 + 4 =$

$7 + 3 =$

$5 + 5 =$

$6 + 2 =$

$4 + 6 =$

$5 + 3 =$

$2 + 7 =$